WONDERS OF THE REPTILE WORLD

DODD, MEAD WONDER BOOKS

Wonders of the Seashore by Jacquelyn Berrill

Wonders of the Woodland Animals by Jacquelyn Berrill

Strange Nurseries by Jacqueline Berrill

Wonders of the Wild by Jacqueline Berrill

Wonders of the Tree World by Margaret Cosgrove

Wonders of Your Senses by Margaret Cosgrove

The Wonders Inside You by Margaret Cosgrove

Wonders Under a Microscope by Margaret Cosgrove

Wonders of the Bird World by Helen Gere Cruickshank

Wonders of the Reptile World by Helen Gere Cruickshank

Wonders of the Heavens by Kenneth Heuer

Wonders of the Aquarium by Sigmund A. Lavine

Wonders of the Ocean Zoo by Boris Arnov, Jr., and Helen Mather-Smith Mindlin

Wonders of the Deep Sea by Boris Arnov, Jr., and Helen Mather-Smith Mindlin

WONDERS OF THE REPTILE WORLD

by

HELEN GERE CRUICKSHANK

illustrations by LON ELLIS

DODD, MEAD and Company • NEW YORK

To the young Gomons, Reggios, Sheehans, Thatchers and Cheryl Cruickshank with a hope that each will have a lifelong series of happy outdoor adventures.

Library of Congress Catalog Card Number: 59-12296
Printed in the United States of America

CONTENTS

ILLUSTRATIONS

The Adventurers with Little Brains

Long after the hot new world had cooled and the oceans separated themselves from the lands, tiny one-celled animals appeared in the warm waters. By the time the world was two billion years old, many one-celled animals had united into colonies that lived together. Slowly these colonies formed many-celled animals of varied sizes and shapes.

Trilobites, corals and sea scorpions became common. Then animals with backbones appeared. Finally fish became common and after them came amphibians which had lungs for part of their lives and could venture onto the land for short visits. But amphibians, like fish, were tied to the water, for their eggs were jellylike and without covering. On land they would quickly dry out and the young life inside would die. They had to be laid in water. When young amphibians hatched, they took oxygen from the water by gills.

About 315 million years ago something wonderful happened. An animal with a backbone laid an egg with a shell to protect it. The egg could be laid on land for the shell kept it from drying out. From that egg came a reptile which breathed air by lungs. It did not have to spend any of its life in the water.

For the first time in the long history of the earth an animal was free of the water. It could live on land. The change from life in the water to life on land was a greater adventure than the crossing of the Atlantic by Columbus or the discovery of the North Pole by Peary or the climbing of Mount Everest by Hilary. It was a greater adventure than the first flight in an airplane by the Wright brothers and greater than the first flight to the moon will be. All those great adventures by man came from plans formed in his big and lively brain. Man does not have to change his body to go on great adventures. He only has to put his mind to work and make great plans.

But reptiles never did have anything but tiny brains. The brains of huge twenty-five-ton reptiles weighed but a few ounces while the brain of a hundred-fifty-pound man may weigh as much as sixty-two ounces. No wonder man can think his way through many wonderful adventures. Reptiles could not think their way out of the water. Nature had to change the bodies of reptiles to fit a new environment, land.

Nobody knows how long it took their bodies to change from water bodies to land bodies. Probably millions of years passed while nature made many, many experiments, discarding this and keeping that until at last the right combination of organs made life on land possible.

During the Mesozoic Era which lasted about 140 million years reptiles were the most numerous animals on earth. That period is often called the Age of Reptiles. Then there were reptiles that ran on two legs, reptiles that walked on four legs and reptiles with no legs at all. Other reptiles had wings and some of those were tiny as sparrows and some had a greater wing spread than any bird.

Some reptiles had no teeth, ate only vegetable matter and swallowed stones which stayed in the gizzard to help grind their food. Some reptiles had huge teeth a foot long and ate only meat. Some were no bigger than mice and some were the biggest animals that ever walked the earth.

The Age of Reptiles ended about sixty million years ago. Since it ended, many new and wonderful animals have taken their place on earth. But today some of the most interesting and wonderful animals alive are relatives of the reptiles of long ago. We should always remember that reptiles were the animals which first adventured onto land and so paved the way for all land animals including man.

The Orders of Living Reptiles

There are so many kinds of animals in the world that scientists separate them into groups which share some important characteristics. They call all animals *reptiles* that have backbones, are covered with scales, breathe air by lungs, and are cold-blooded.

About five thousand living species or kinds of animals fit in the reptile group. These are divided into orders. In past ages there were many more kinds of reptiles than there are today. By studying their fossil remains as well as the living reptiles, scientists have made nineteen reptile orders. Of these, fifteen orders of reptiles no longer live. The four orders of living reptiles are:

1. Crocodilians. There are about twenty-five species of these. They are seldom found beyond the tropics.

2. Beakheads. Only one species, the tuatara, is alive today. During the Reptile Age beakheads were fairly common.

3. Turtles. About three hundred species. Some live on land, others spend most of their lives in water. Turtles are the most ancient reptiles living today. There were turtles before there were dinosaurs.

4. Lizards and snakes. About 2,500 lizards and 2,000 snakes are known but new species are often discovered. Of all living reptiles snakes are the youngest form and venture farthest from the tropics.

A reptile, says the dictionary, is an animal that crawls on its belly or on short legs. This does not tell the whole story. To be sure, all snakes and a few lizards have no legs. Crocodilians may lazily slide off a bank into the water without standing up but they walk with the body and tail held well off the ground. Some lizards run on their strong hind legs. It takes more than a crawling motion to make a reptile.

The fact that reptiles are cold-blooded is often misunderstood. Except for birds and mammals, all animals in the world are cold-blooded. Reptiles do not feel cold and slimy. But they do not have a heating system in their bodies that keeps their temperature at a certain degree. Their temperature is almost as cold or almost as hot as the air, water or earth around them.

Unless you are sick, your temperature is about 98.6 degrees. But remember that among mammals that hibernate, temperature is not always the same. The temperature of a hibernating woodchuck may fall almost to freezing.

Many thrushes have a temperature of about 112 degrees. But very young thrushes must be sheltered by their parents, for their heating systems do not begin to work as soon as they hatch. Unless they are sheltered they may become too hot or too cold and die. To be cold-blooded is not as strange and unpleasant as you thought!

Because they cannot keep a steady body temperature and therefore prefer a warm climate, reptiles are most common in or near the tropics. They do not go high on great mountains for it is too cold there. They do not live in polar regions for the same reason. The most hardy reptile cannot live where the ground is frozen all year. When cold weather comes, a reptile must burrow in the earth or find a good hole in the rocks or a hollow tree where it can hibernate until warm days come again.

Giants in the Rocks

The War of 1812 had ended and Americans had settled down to a peaceful life when in 1818 strange tracks were discovered in the Connecticut River Valley. They were large and printed deep in the rocks. People came from miles around to look at them with awe. To be sure, fossils had been discovered before in many parts of the world. Except for scientists, most people did not understand them and believed they simply proved that the account of the Great Flood in the Bible was true and nothing more. Many who stared at the great fossil footprints in those Connecticut rocks believed they must be tracks made by the raven when Noah released it from the Ark.

Scientists knew those rocks were far more ancient than most people realized and even more exciting than any of those who stared at the tracks imagined. The tracks told scientists that once unknown giant animals had walked the earth. Eagerly they studied the tracks and searched in other places for more, and for bones of animals long gone from the earth. Soon they began to discover and carefully dig up great numbers of fossil bones. Painstakingly they fitted the bones together and finally they were able to understand much about those giant animals of long ago.

Within a few years so many fossils of ancient species of reptiles had been found that scientists began to separate them into orders. The word "dinosaur," which means "terrible lizard," was invented for a group of fossil reptiles which were most abundant and included some of the biggest and most terrible animals that ever lived on land. Because scientists have studied so many fossils of bygone animals and plants and the traces of ancient seas, rivers, lakes and mountains, we now have tiny glimpses of the world of long ago. Those glimpses into the past are like dreams without color, for fossils give us no clue to the colors of those ancient reptiles.

If we could go back in time about 315 million years we would see the world as it looked when the first reptile crawled out of the sea to live on land. It was a strange world. There was not a flowering plant or tree anywhere. Though there were great forests, all the trees would be strange to us. Cycads looking as they do today would be the only plants we would recognize. Perhaps insects would bite us for they were already common in that far-off time.

Leaping forward some 85 million years we would find ourselves at the beginning of the Age of Reptiles when reptiles were common and dinosaurs were kings of the earth. The Age of Reptiles lasted throughout the Mesozoic Era, which began about 200 million years ago and spanned 140 million years. We realize what a long time reptiles were kings when we stop to think man has been king of the earth for just a few thousand years.

About the time the first flowering plants appeared and many dinosaurs had developed strange armor-plated skins and great horns, while others had grown to fantastic sizes, they suddenly began to die out. Soon the dinosaurs were gone from the world forever. Many other strange reptiles including the pterosaurs disappeared too.

Scientists do not agree about the cause of the sudden disappearance of so many kinds of reptiles. They disappeared at a time when the earth was changing. Mountains were rising and falling. Earthquakes shook the earth and volcanoes sent out molten lava and perhaps deadly gases. The seas were changing positions. No doubt shallow waters and great swamps where the plant-loving dinosaurs fed were suddenly drained so the reptiles starved. Meat-eating dinosaurs were not able to travel quickly enough to other feeding grounds and they too starved. Dinosaurs may have grown too big and too specialized to live in a changing world.

Whatever the reason for dying, the bodies of some sank into the mud. Sand drifted over others. Gradually they were buried deeper and deeper. When conditions were just right throughout the entire reptile age, some of the bodies were pressed into stone and became what we call fossils.

The fossils lay undisturbed for millions of years. Occasionally one was washed out of the rocks by a spring flood. But little attention was given to those strange records of the past until after the discovery of the dinosaur tracks in the rocks of the Connecticut River valley.

Though dinosaur fossils have been found in most parts of the world, the western United States is believed to have the most dinosaur fossils as well as the greatest number of species. Once it must have been the capital of the dinosaurs, the reptile kings of the world!

Today people travel thousands of miles to visit Dinosaur National Monument lying on the Green River partly in Colorado and partly in Utah. In this National Monument is a genuine buried treasure of dinosaur fossil riches. We are fortunate that this fossil treasure which tells so much about the Age of Reptiles is preserved for all people to enjoy.

Dinosaurs, Kings of the Reptile Age

At the beginning of the Mesozoic Era, dinosaurs, the terrible lizards, had taken their place in the growing family of reptiles. The first dinosaurs all walked on their hind legs. The most ancient ones yet discovered were about the size of hens but as time went on the dinosaurs became more varied in form. They also grew bigger and bigger until some of them became the largest animals that ever walked the earth. Beside some of the biggest dinosaurs, an elephant would be a pigmy weighing but a fifth as much.

The small dinosaurs were every bit as strange and interesting as the giant species. But when we go to a museum to see fossil dinosaur bones and restorations which show us how those great animals of long ago must have looked, we like best to look at the huge species, not the small ones.

The first dinosaurs walked on their hind legs but many later species walked on all four legs. Some ate only meat and some ate vegetable matter and some ate a little of both. Because their food needs varied, the teeth of some were very large, some had small teeth and a few had no teeth at all. Since they were cold-blooded animals they did not have to eat as much or as often as do warm-blooded mammals and birds.

Some dinosaurs may have reached ninety feet or more in length. They became about a third as long as a city block. A few may have weighed almost fifty tons. A Brachiosaurus thigh bone six feet long has been found. Think how tiny a six-foot man would look beside that great Brachiosaurus. How the earth must have trembled and shaken when such a giant walked.

When we consider dinosaurs as small as a hen and others ninety feet long and weighing as much as a trailer truck, and remember that there were all sizes of dinosaurs from the tiny ones to the huge ones, and that some walked on two legs and some on four legs, we begin to realize what a great and varied group of reptiles the dinosaurs were.

Struthiomimus

Struthiomimus was twice as long as a man is tall. It measured about twelve feet from the tip of its toothless horny jaws to the end of its tail. It walked on strong hind legs and could run with great swiftness. Like birds today, it stood on its toes with the rest of its feet high off the ground. Its feet looked so much like those of a rhea, the American ostrich, that some scientists believe Struthiomimus was the ancestor of those birds. Unlike birds, which all have feathers, Struthiomimus was covered with a scaly skin.

Though the hind legs of Struthiomimus were good running legs, its forelegs were slender and quite small. Probably the forelegs never rested on the ground and were only used for pulling down branches or digging up plants. Each foreleg had three slender fingers which ended in long curved pointed claws. These could not be twisted about as our fingers can. They could only be opened and closed.

Struthiomimus had a very small head and a tiny brain but its eyes were large. Since its neck was long, slender, and moved freely, perhaps the dinosaur could twist it enough to see if an enemy approached from behind. No doubt it depended on its eyes to discover danger and on its strong hind legs to carry it swiftly to a safe place.

Struthiomimus

Tyrannosaurus Rex, the Tyrant King

Of all carnivorous land animals that ever lived, Tyrannosaurus rex was probably the largest and most terrible. It had an all-over length of almost forty-five feet. It walked, like Struthiomimus, only on its hind legs, but what a contrast it was to that slender horny-beaked dinosaur. Tyrannosaurus was three times as tall as a six-foot man as it raced over the countryside after its prey, which it probably followed by scent as a dog follows a rabbit. How terrified the victims of its chase must have been as Tyrannosaurus overtook them.

Not only were the claws on its powerful hind legs long, sharp, and curved but so were those on its quite short and slender forelegs. Its blunt jaws gaped to show double pointed teeth almost a foot long.

It is believed that Tyrannosaurus ate nothing but meat, which it captured easily for it ran swiftly with its great tail held off the ground to balance its heavy body. With its huge teeth it could slash many an animal in half with a single snap of its powerful jaws.

People visiting a museum who see a restoration of a Tyrannosaurus rex towering high above them sometimes feel as if they are looking at the kind of animal they dream of in a nightmare. No wonder scientists call this huge, powerful dinosaur "the tyrant king." Even a saber-toothed tiger was not nearly as big and powerful as Tyrannosaurus.

Tyrannosaurus and Stegosaurus

Brontosaurus, the Thunder Reptile

When Brontosaurus the Thunder Reptile walked, the marshy ground where it liked to feed must have trembled at each step. Probably this dinosaur weighed about twenty-five tons. Some were as much as seventy-five feet long. Though Brontosaurus was not quite the largest land animal that ever walked the earth (Brachiosaurus probably wears that crown) it is one of the best known dinosaurs, for it was quite abundant in America and many museums have fossil skeletons or restorations of it.

Brontosaurus walked on all four legs. It had a huge barrel-like body and a very long thick tail which ended in a whiplike tip. Its neck was very long and on top of this perched a silly little head in which was housed a very tiny brain. Probably Brontosaurus knew little more than enough to eat when hungry.

This great dinosaur must have spent most of its life in shallow water. Since it had few teeth and those were small, it ate soft juicy plants growing in ponds. We know it preferred that habitat, for most Brontosaurus fossils are found in rocks that formed where once there were swamps and ponds. Perhaps the water which supported their massive bodies helped to rest their weary legs.

As this is written a shiny red stone weighing eleven ounces lies beside the typewriter. The stone feels very smooth and a little oily. It is a gizzard stone. Long ago it was swallowed by a Brontosaurus to help grind its food just as birds today swallow gravel for the same purpose. Gravel was far too small to help a Brontosaurus. Some stones they swallowed were as heavy as any a boy would choose to throw.

Brontosaurus

Many dinosaur fossils have been found with stones clustered as in a nest where the gizzard must have been. As many as 116 gizzard stones have been found in a single dinosaur fossil. Naturally only those dinosaurs with small teeth or no teeth at all had gizzard stones. Apparently when the gizzard stones were worn so smooth they no longer helped grind food, the dinosaurs regurgitated or spat them out. After handling many, many gizzard stones, scientists can recognize them even when they no longer lie within the fossil skeleton.

Some vertebrae of Brontosaurus were as much as four and a half feet high. This is bigger than any whale vertebra. No doubt when Tyrannosaurus was really hungry it did not hesitate to attack and kill a thunder reptile. Brontosaurus was too heavy to run away and escape the swift and powerful Tyrannosaurus. Brontosaurus was too big for its own good.

Two Armored Dinosaurs: Triceratops and Stegosaurus

As the Reptile Age drew toward its end, still other strange and wonderful dinosaurs became common. These are called by scientists the armored or plated reptiles. For their protection, nature invented many kinds of armor made of bone.

Most people have seen horned lizards and handled them. If a queer little horned lizard could suddenly puff itself up until its body was as big as an elephant and its head was six feet long, it would resemble somewhat the dinosaur Triceratops.

Triceratops walked on all four legs. It had a horn on the tip of its snout and another over each eye. On the back of its head was a great frill made of bone plates. Scientists believe the frill helped to balance the forepart of its head which carried those three great heavy horns.

As long as Triceratops could swing about to face an enemy it must have been a match for almost any creature, even Tyrannosaurus. Its armor kept it safe from slashing teeth.

Of all the armored dinosaurs, Stegosaurus was the strangest. Some of them measured thirty feet in length. Its tiny head was drawn into a blunt point. Its tail was rather short and blunt too. Near the tip of the tail two or three sharp horns three feet long stood upright. On its back, Stegosaurus had queer big bonelike plates standing along each side of the spine. Some of these were as much as three feet wide and three feet high but they were quite thin except near the skin. They broke all rules of animal structure by being arranged alternately instead of opposite each other.

Stegosaurus walked on all four rather elephantlike stubby legs. It was quite flattened from side to side. If it approached head on it looked quite thin, but if seen from the side it looked very big and broad.

Scientists believe Stegosaurus ate only vegetable matter. They think too that it descended from a kind of dinosaur that walked only on its hind legs. But as the armorlike plates became bigger and bigger their weight finally was too great for the hind legs alone and Stegosaurus let its forelegs drop to the ground and take half the load.

Most Stegosaurus fossils are found in Wyoming and Colorado. The last one to live must have had its final meal of leaves about sixty million years ago.

Once we begin to know a little about the wonders of animal life long before man took his place on earth, we can never take a walk without looking for traces of the past. We always look with interested eyes at each living reptile we see for they are relatives of the long-ago kings of the Reptile Age.

Dragons of the Air

During the Mesozoic Era some reptiles learned to fly. Scientists call the flying reptiles pterosaurs (the *p* is silent when you pronounce "ptero-saur" and "pteranodon"). By the middle of the Mesozoic there were swarms of pterosaurs. Some were no bigger than tree swallows. Probably

Draco (Flying Dragon) and Pterodactyl Ptarodon

they chased and caught insects as swallows do today. But they were not covered with feathers as birds are. Their skin was covered with scales.

Some pterosaurs had long thin tails, some had short tails and some had no tails at all. It is believed that some of them flew at night as owls do, for their fossil remains tell us they had very large eyes.

Pterosaurs were a marvel of lightness. The wing bones of the biggest species were little thicker than a sheet of blotting paper. Some pterosaurs had big crests on the back of the head which must have helped balance their massive beaks. Some had smooth heads. Some species had small but very sharp teeth.

The wings of pterosaurs were formed of the arm and thin skin which could be opened for flight or folded when at rest. In most species the little finger was extremely long and this was turned toward the hind legs when the wing was folded.

The wings varied greatly in form. Some pterosaurs had flaps which stretched only over the hand and arm. In other species the flap of skin was attached to the body as well as the arm and hand. In still others it extended to the hind legs and even across the base of the tail. No doubt flight among the many species varied from a mere glide to flight as expert as that of birds and bats in other species. Some pterodons had a greater wing spread than any living birds.

The largest known pterosaur is called pteranodon. It had a wing spread of almost twenty feet. It is believed this great creature weighed less than twenty pounds. Wandering albatrosses have the greatest wing spread of any bird in the world yet they seldom measure twelve feet from one wing tip to the other. In spite of their much smaller wing spread, wandering albatrosses probably are as heavy as the much bigger pterodons were.

By the end of the Reptile Age the pterosaurs were no more. Fortunately they left many fossils in the rocks as records of their life during that vast period of time called the Mesozoic.

The flying reptiles of today are harmless little lizards which seldom grow longer than ten inches. The family of flying lizards is called Draco, which means "dragon." Several species of these flying dragons are found in southeast Asia and the East Indies.

With the flying dragons nature made a strange experiment. Some of the ribs of Draco have become enormously long. A thin skin covers them. Flying dragons cannot fly as many pterosaurs did nor can they fly as birds and bats do today. They can only glide on their rib-wings, but this they do expertly. They make long glides from tree to tree. When they land, the wings are folded tightly against their sides.

There is a touch of magic about flying dragons. In flight they look as bright and beautiful as butterflies. When they land and fold their wings, all the gay colors suddenly disappear.

If you prepared a cage for some flying dragons and placed it in a cluster of branches, you could enjoy a real magic show. When placed in their new cage, the flying dragons would hurry around exploring their new home. But leave them alone for a while and then return. The cage seems empty of animals. You fear the new pets have escaped. Now look more closely. Suddenly you discover a slight swelling on one of the twigs. It is a flying dragon which has found a twig to its liking and stretched itself along its chosen perch. Its wings are folded close to its sides. Its legs are tucked against its body and its tail and chin lie flat on the twig. Its soft color matches the twig. All the bright colors of its wings are hidden. The flying dragon has become invisible. Slowly you discover the rest of your flying dragons. Each one is in plain sight yet they are almost as invisible as a bewitched hero in a fairy tale.

Hundreds of millions of years ago nature experimented with flying reptiles. The pterosaurs all disappeared by the end of the Reptile Age. Now Draco lizards, the flying dragons of today, glide easily from tree to tree on a new kind of wings made of elongated ribs.

When we read of the golden tree snake of south Asiatic islands which flattens itself and then glides gently to the ground, and when we see green anoles of the United States leap from the top of a fence or the limb of a tree to the ground many feet below and run away unharmed, we cannot help wondering if nature is preparing to make still more experiments with flight in the strange world of reptiles.

The Crocodilians

Today crocodilians are the largest, most powerful reptiles on earth. They are not happy except in warm climates. Those living farthest from the equator hibernate in their "holes" or dens when it grows cold. Except for two alligators, one living in China and one in the United States, crocodilians are found only in or near the tropics.

While crocodilians are most numerous in Africa and Asia, South America has nine or ten species, which is the most found on any continent. Columbia may be called the crocodilian capital of the world, for it has seven native species.

Twenty-five species of crocodilians are known to scientists. They are divided into groups called alligators, caimans, gavials and crocodiles. Many of them look so much alike that only a scientist can tell them apart.

Crocodilians with very long, very narrow snouts are called gavials. Gavials have a funny soft knob on the tip of the snout which can be inflated like a little balloon. Gavials eat little but fish.

Crocodiles have rather pointed snouts but they are not nearly as narrow as those of the gavial. Fish is their chief food. Crocodiles are considered the most dangerous of all the crocodilians.

Both alligators and caimans have fairly broad, rounded snouts. They look so much alike that it is difficult to tell which is which even when lying side by side in a zoo. Their diet is more varied than that of gavials and crocodiles.

All crocodilians have powerful jaws and big teeth. Strangely enough, the great jaws which snap shut like a steel trap open weakly.

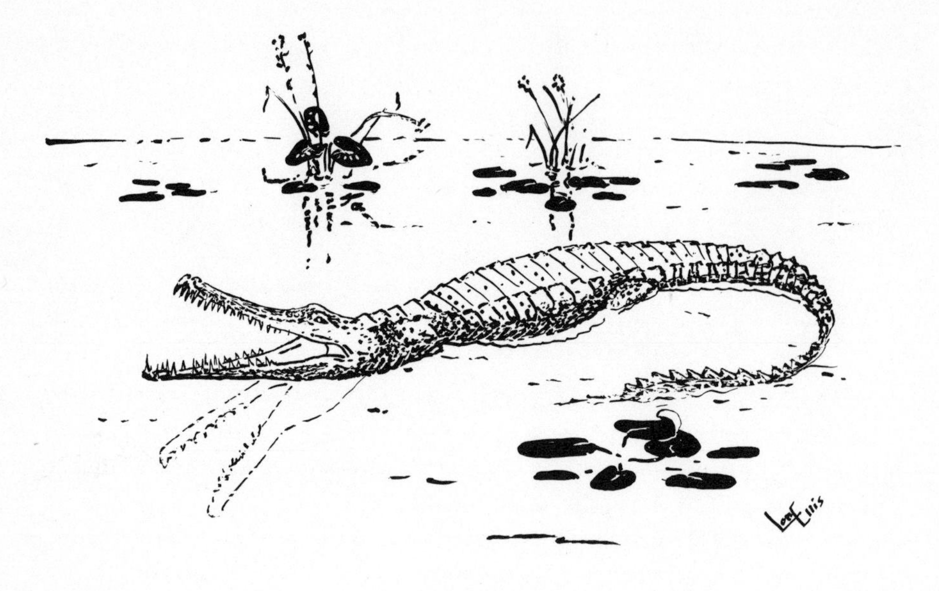

Gavial

Crocodilians delight in sun-bathing on banks beside water. They often lie with their huge jaws wide open. In Africa crocodile birds feed among basking crocodiles and sometimes enter the great pink mouths to pick parasites from around the teeth.

The skull bones of crocodilians are so thick that an enemy cannot find a place to attack. If the head is strong as a fort, the tail is a destroyer. It is long, muscular and powerful. With a swift side-swipe, crocodilians can knock a man and many other large animals off their feet. Then the lazy, sluggish-looking crocodilian turns in a flash and seizes the unbalanced creature.

In the water, the tail acts as a propeller. When the animal swims, the short legs are folded against the body and the tail moves rhythmically from side to side, pushing the crocodilian through the water as fast as a fish can swim.

The scaly skin is very tough. Horny scales set in rows along the back are reinforced with bone plates. Even the belly scales have a reinforcement of small bone plates.

Most crocodilians average less than twelve feet in length. But both

American and Orinoco crocodiles have reached twenty-three feet. Salt-water crocodiles are not far behind these monsters in extreme measurements.

The tails of crocodilians are in great demand as food in many parts of the world. Man also seeks crocodilians for their valuable skins. Many people are afraid of big crocodilians and kill them whenever they can. Since man is armed with high-powered guns he is the most dangerous enemy crocodilians have.

In the United States the approach of a child is usually enough to send a basking alligator or crocodile dashing into the safety of the water. They are afraid of man. They do not appear dangerous at all.

This is not true in all parts of the world. In Africa and India where crocodiles are abundant, it is said that many natives are eaten by these reptiles. Records over a period of twenty-five years in Ceylon show that 53 people were eaten by salt-water crocodiles.

In some countries crocodiles have been used as a sort of lie-detector. Men accused of a crime have been forced to swim in crocodile-infested waters. The final judgment was not based on truth, but on how hungry the crocodiles were!

Although American crocodilians generally hide from man, a female guarding her nest will attack an intruder fiercely. She will fight against great odds to protect her eggs and young. All crocodilians are dangerous if wounded or cornered. As a rule, however, only people who are careless or who do stupid things are harmed by crocodilians native to the United States.

Crocodilians are scarce in this country. To be sure, alligator farms are common in Florida. But the sight of hundreds of crocodilians lying on a cement-floored pen is not half as exciting as the unexpected sight of one in its natural home. With luck you may one day see what appears to be an old log lying in the water. Suddenly you realize the log is alive. Nostrils on the end of the snout stick above the surface. Perhaps a bit of the back and tail may be seen. You have discovered a reptile left over from ancient days when dinosaurs roamed the earth. How wonderful it is that some wild crocodilians live and grow up in the wilds. We wish everybody could have the thrill of finding in its wilderness home, a crocodilian, a member of the family that holds the title, "the world's biggest reptiles."

The American Alligator

American alligators are found in swampy places and many lakes and rivers in the southeastern United States. Except for a Chinese alligator this brave species is the only crocodilian in the world that ventures far into the temperate zone.

Alligators are the heaviest, stockiest species of crocodilians. One eleven-foot six-inch 'gator weighed a quarter of a ton. The longest accurately measured American alligator reached nineteen and a half feet but they average only eight to ten feet.

On land an alligator is clumsy enough so a man may easily avoid it. In the water the 'gator is the swifter, more agile animal. It can bite easily under water, for a flap of skin closes the throat and keeps out the water. Except when cornered or defending eggs or young, there are few records of 'gators attacking man.

It is fortunate that alligators seldom do attack man for they have a powerful bite. A large 'gator can crush the bones of a full grown cow. A Louisiana man who kept many alligators in captivity teased one until it bit on a steel plate. It bit so hard that one of its teeth was pushed through its skull and had to be pulled out with pliers.

When spring approaches, alligators begin to bellow in southern swamps. The sound is a deep booming roar. On a still night the roar of a big bull 'gator carries for a mile or more. The marsh seems to vibrate with the sound so it is felt almost more than heard. It is a stirring and wonderful sound to hear in the wilderness.

A female alligator builds a large nest by first clearing an area about five feet in diameter. It swings its tail about, knocking over plants. Then it tramples them and drags its body across them until everything is to its liking. Next, trash is piled up. The 'gator uses her mouth to gather some of this but her body movements shove most of it into a heap. When the pile is about two feet high, she flattens the top by crawling over it. Finally she makes a hollow in the center and drops anywhere from twenty-five to seventy eggs in it. The heat of the sun and decay-

Alligator

ing vegetation keep the eggs warm while the young 'gators develop. If the female does not protect the nest with care, it will surely be robbed by a hungry bear, raccoon, skunk or other creature. Even man likes the eggs and steals them when he can.

Young 'gators begin to call before they hatch. Usually the mother hears them, opens the nest and when they have hatched leads the young to water. Then fish, turtles, birds and many other animals try to catch and eat them. Not until they become big and powerful are alligators safe from their hungry neighbors.

Alligators generally have a favorite den. Sometimes they use a safe place made by nature. More often they dig their own dens. Some of these are forty feet long. Alligators hibernate in them during the winter months. They also hurry into them when danger threatens.

Alligators have very large stomachs. One 'gator not quite twelve feet long once swallowed one after another three whole pigs each weighing about thirty pounds. Though they sometimes eat huge meals in summer, they eat little or nothing from October until late March.

Alligators are shot in many places but they are safe in the Audubon Sanctuaries, Everglades National Park, in Florida State Parks and in United States Fish and Wildlife Refuges. They are scarce in many of their old-time haunts and their numbers are greatly reduced from what they were at the beginning of this century. But we may be sure they will not be destroyed in their sanctuaries by their worst enemy, man. Some will remain for us to enjoy.

The American Crocodile

One day in 1875 William T. Hornaday, the great zoologist, was exploring Biscayne Bay. There was no Miami skyline then. In fact, not a single white person lived within many miles of the Bay. He was in an area of shallow waters and dense mangrove thickets where Seminole Indians occasionally came to fish or hunt.

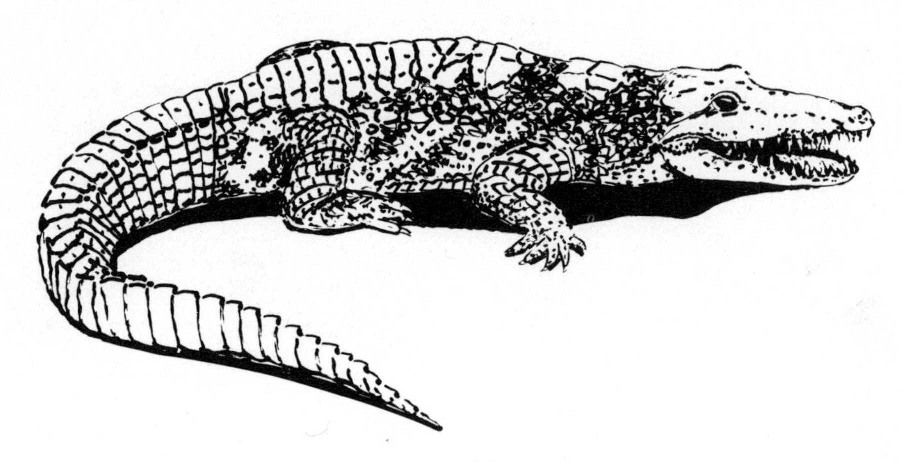

Crocodile

Suddenly he saw a crocodile. It was the first one ever discovered by a scientist north of Mexico. Though four inches of its tail were missing, the crocodile measured fourteen feet two inches from its snout to the end of its chewed-off tail.

Today crocodiles in the United States are found only on the very tip of Florida and the Florida Keys. Their average length is between ten and twelve feet. They are more slender and quick than alligators and their snouts are more pointed. Also they are more vicious. It is said the young ones will bite as soon as they open their shells.

Young crocodiles, like all crocodilians, have an egg tooth on the tip of the snout. With this they weaken the shell at hatching time. The egg tooth falls off soon after the young emerge. From the moment they hatch, the small black-marked greenish crocodiles take care of themselves but as with 'gators, if the mothers are not attentive, many are eaten by their animal neighbors.

Americans seldom see crocodiles in their wilderness homes. Occasionally the owner of a fishing camp in southern Florida or on the Keys has protected a crocodile and it has learned to act as a garbage disposer by eating the heads and entrails thrown into the water when fish are cleaned. Then people come from all parts of the country and wait for many hours in the hope of seeing a genuine wild crocodile in its natural home.

Tuatara, the Three-eyed Beakhead

In 1831 the one and only living beakhead was discovered. Until that time beakheads were known only as ancient reptiles, fairly common in the Mesozoic, judging by the numbers of fossils scientists discovered. No record remains of how the wonderful discovery of a living beakhead was made. Perhaps it happened somewhat this way. An assistant may have come to a scientist on an expedition to New Zealand and said,

"Here is the day's collection of animals. We had very good luck and collected some new lizards along the rocks on the shore."

No doubt the scientist examined the new reptiles with interest and the assistant, proud of his knowledge of the native Maori language, may have said, "The Maoris call those tautaras. *Tua* means 'back' and *tara* means 'spines.' Notice the spines all along the backbone and on the back of the head, but there are none on the neck."

The scientist picked up one of the olive-green reptiles with pale yellow specks on its sides and looked at the yellow spines along the back. We may be sure he examined it with care while the assistant went back to his work.

Presently the scientist exclaimed with excitement, "This reptile is not a lizard!"

The assistant grinned and joked, "Well, it isn't a turtle and it isn't a crocodilian. If it isn't a lizard, you must think it is the world's only snake with legs."

But the scientist replied seriously, "It should be a fossil, dead and buried a hundred million years ago. The skull bones prove it is not a lizard. It is a beakhead. It has always been believed that all species of beakheads died out at the same time dinosaurs vanished from the earth. This is one of the most wonderful animal discoveries of modern times."

Almost a century and a half has passed since our imaginary conversation about the beakhead in New Zealand. Now the whole world has been explored by scientists. In all the world no other member of the once great order of beakheads has been discovered. The tuatara is the only beakhead species still living. Its closest known relatives lived in Europe some 135 million years ago. With the single exception of the tuatara, all the beakheads are as dead as the dinosaurs.

During the Mesozoic, beakheads were fairly common. They were never as numerous as the dinosaurs nor did any species ever grow to be as large as some of those kings of the reptile age. How the single species reached New Zealand and managed to survive to this day is one of the mysteries of the reptile world.

What a strange reptile the tuatara is! Of all living reptiles, its life processes are the slowest. In fact, they are slower than those of any other vertebrate, slower than those of amphibians, fish or the wormlike chordates. Sometimes a healthy tuatara will show no sign of breathing for a whole hour at a time.

Some people call the tuatara the three-eyed monster. It is not much of a monster but when it is young it truly does have a third eye on the top of its head. This eye has a lens and a retina but no iris. Like all reptile eyes, it is covered with a transparent scale. As the tuatara grows older this scale becomes cloudy and inconspicuous. Tuataras no longer see through the third eye, though it is believed this eye is sensitive to light.

African Chameleons and a Tuatara

Tuataras seldom grow longer than thirty inches. They weigh about two pounds. It is not known how long they generally live but one was kept alive in the Dublin zoo for thirty-three years.

Once tuataras were quite common in New Zealand but as Europeans settled there they brought along dogs, cats, foxes, sheep and pigs. They also brought along rats though they did not mean to do that. Some of these animals killed the tuataras and others ate the white, one-inch-long eggs. Sheep, goats and other farm animals ate the vegetation where the tuataras lived and liked to hide. Rapidly the tuataras began to disappear. Soon they could be found only on rocky islands off the coast. Just in time the New Zealand government began to protect their habitat. All domestic animals were taken off the islands where tuataras still lived. The plants began to grow again. With the return of natural plant growth, the tuataras again had a suitable home. Now the tuataras, the last of the beakheads, live in the safety of a sanctuary provided by the government of New Zealand.

On their protected islands the tuataras lay their eggs, sometimes as many as fourteen, in burrows or in rocky crevices. Sometimes they dig their own burrows. Sometimes they use burrows dug by petrels, little birds of the ocean that never come to land except to make their nest burrow, lay a single egg, and rear the young bird.

Tuataras feed mostly at night. They eat insects, slugs, snails, earthworms and even small mammals such as mice. They stalk their prey and then catch it with a sudden lunge.

The race of three-eyed tuataras has survived unchanged for a hundred million years. It is the only beakhead to live beyond the Age of Reptiles. After having lived as a race for millions of years, it came close to sudden extinction when white men came to New Zealand. We are thankful that this living treasure from the Mesozoic Era now has a sanctuary where it may live its slow, strange life undisturbed.

Turtles

Whenever you see a turtle you know it is a turtle. With a shell on top and bottom, with a beaked mouth and no teeth, and with four stout legs you recognize a turtle wherever you meet one. Of all reptiles, the turtle order is the easiest to recognize. Young crocodilians may look like lizards, some lizards may look like snakes, but turtles look only like turtles.

Turtles have lived on earth for more than three hundred million years. Before there were dinosaurs, turtles performed the marvelous feat of pushing their ribs outside their legs to form the plastron or undershell. The upper shell or carapace begins to grow along the backbone and soon pushes in all directions. Turtles seem to enjoy having their shells scratched gently.

Turtles reached their greatest variety and size in the far-off Mesozoic. Fossils of a marine turtle called Archelon which measured more than twelve feet in length and may have weighed a ton have been found in South Dakota.

Today the largest species of turtle, the leatherback, may reach nine feet in length and weigh as much as 1,500 pounds. Such sea giants are very scarce. Unfortunately when one is discovered it is almost surely captured and killed.

Of all reptiles, turtles live the longest. It is believed they live longer than any other backboned animal, including man. Five species of turtles have lived for a century or more in captivity.

Great size in a turtle does not mean great age. A twelve-year-old leatherback may weigh 350 pounds. Galápagos turtles are favorites in zoos. One of these weighing twenty-nine pounds when it was delivered at a zoo became a 350-pound heavyweight in seven years. Turtles usually mature between three and seven years. Before maturity they grow very fast. After they mature the rate of growth becomes slower and slower the older they grow.

There are pigmies as well as giants among turtles. In the United States bog turtles seldom reach a length of three and a half inches.

A few species of turtles see colors almost as well as man. This is quite remarkable. We take color for granted but most animals see the world in tones of black, gray and white. While birds, apes and man see colors, dogs, cats and sheep are color-blind. Even bulls, which are supposed to be angered by red, actually are enraged by the movement of the toreador's cape, not by its color.

Turtles, which have no external ears, hear poorly or not at all. They respond to vibrations in the water or land. Because they do not hear it is strange that mating sea turtles can be heard for a half mile on still nights. They groan, hiss and bellow. Many turtles hiss when frightened.

Most turtles have a keen sense of smell. No doubt this helps them find food. The same sense may help them find others of their kind, for some give off a strong odor. In the United States one of these is the musk turtle.

Musk turtles spend most of their lives crawling on the bottom of ponds and streams. Fortunately they are small for their necks are long, their jaws are strong and they have bad tempers. They should be handled with great caution. Musk turtles have two scent gland openings on each side of the body where the skin meets the upper shell or carapace. They exude the scent when handled. This is so disagreeable that one species of musk turtle is called the stinkpot.

Turtles appear to enjoy the sun. Sea turtles far from land often float on top of the water. Fresh-water turtles climb on logs, stumps or rocks to sun-bathe. It is amusing to see how suddenly a sun bath ends when a boat approaches. All the turtles crawl or fall into the water with a splash and disappear. Turtles do not begin to need as much oxygen as do warm-blooded animals. Therefore they can hold their breaths for a long time.

No turtle in the world has teeth. Instead they have a horny rim on powerful jaws. The jaws are a real pair of choppers. Food is digested slowly and turtles may fast for months. Many species eat both plant and animal life. Some eat carrion.

While turtles eat many kinds of animals, many creatures eat not only turtles but their eggs also. Usually turtles lay eggs but once a year. Sea turtles crawl ashore at high tide and with their flippers make holes in the sand beyond the reach of the tide. There they lay their white eggs, then scrape sand over them and erase the marks of the nesting place. Loggerhead turtles have been known to lay as many as two hundred eggs in a single nest, but fifty is a more usual number.

Because so many animals like turtle eggs, sea turtles have disappeared from many places where once they were common. Now it is illegal for people to take sea turtle eggs but raccoons, birds, bears and other animals do not know this.

Fresh-water turtles and land turtles never lay as many eggs as the biggest, oldest sea turtles. One African turtle (Tornier's) lays only one egg each year.

The Green Turtle

Green turtles range the warm oceans of the entire world. A few occasionally follow the warm Gulf Stream northward. Some have actually gone as far as northern Europe. But most of these adventurers leave the Gulf Stream earlier and straggle toward the chilly shores as far north as New England. Usually such cold, lost turtles are caught by fishermen and soon die.

In the warm oceans thousands of green turtles are captured every year for market. Most weigh between fifty and two hundred pounds though there is a record of one 850-pound giant.

The name "green turtle" comes not from the color of their shell but from their fat, which has a greenish tint. Usually their carapace is a smooth polished light brown but as they swim toward the surface of the sea they look quite yellow.

Green Turtle

Green turtles, like all sea turtles, must come to the surface to breathe. They let out the air with a sharp hiss. Then they take a long slow breath and may sink immediately beneath the surface.

When over fishing banks off Florida it is amusing to watch terns, which do not like to settle on the water. Whenever a green turtle rises to the surface, a tern usually hovers above it with its legs hanging ready to land on the turtle's back if it decides to bask. When the sun is hot and the water is calm, sea turtles may float for hours, apparently basking as happily as do their fresh-water relatives.

As green turtles are taken by thousands every year from the sea, they are placed on their backs. The undershell or plastron is without support. Therefore unless the turtle, so perfectly adapted to life in the sea, is placed on its back, its great weight will force the air from its lungs and it will die. Lying on their backs, green turtles can live for a week or more on deck.

Though their weight presses the air from their lungs, and their flippers so useful for swimming are very feeble on land, green turtles must go ashore to lay their eggs. Once a year the females slowly drag themselves across a sandy beach, scrape a hole and lay their eggs.

The eggs hatch by themselves. When they hatch, the two-inch-long green turtles claw their way out of the sand and move toward the sea. Many never reach it for birds and other animals eat them. Many that reach the water are snapped up by fish. A few lucky ones escape to grow up and lay eggs of their own.

The Diamondback Turtle

A flock of white ibis settled to the ground under the mangroves. They walked up and down, then gathered in a little group and probed in

Diamondback Turtle

the ground with their long red bills. They had found and were eating the eggs of diamondback turtles. They could find the nests where not a mark was visible to human eyes. Many creatures including man like to eat the eggs of diamondback turtles but few can find them as well as white ibis.

Diamondback turtles belong to the coast. They live in salt marshes, in shallow lagoons and quiet bays. They like the mangrove thickets along southern shores.

These small turtles seldom grow longer than eight inches. Once their delicious flesh was so highly prized that diamondback turtles almost disappeared. Now the fashion for eating them has waned and the turtles, once near extinction, are becoming fairly common in parts of their coastal habitat.

If you visit their favorite habitat on a warm day in May and sit there quietly, you may see a diamondback turtle come out of the shallow waters, thump about until the right place is found, then dig its hole and lay its eggs. When the eggs are covered and the diamondback has returned to the water, you will marvel at the skill with which the nest was hidden. Though you know exactly where it is, you cannot see a single trace of it.

The Snapping Turtle

Fresh-water turtles have odd names. Different groups are called saw-backs, sliders, cooters and stinkers. None has a more appropriate name than the snapping turtle. It really snaps. The snapping turtle is the best known of the fresh-water species. It is found in suitable places from the Atlantic to the Rocky Mountains.

Snapping turtles have a small plastron, a long saw-toothed tail and a big ugly-looking head with savage jaws. Big individuals weigh as much as thirty-five pounds.

Snappers rarely bask. On land they are savage and should be ap-

Snapping Turtle

proached with care. Their necks are long and they can strike some distance with their powerful jaws. Sometimes they rise on their hind quarters and lunge forward with open jaws.

Snapping turtles eat almost any animal food of suitable size they can find on land or in the water. They also eat some plant material. Sometimes a snapper enters a fish hatchery or duck farm where food is abundant. Usually the angry owner quickly kills it. Since snappers are useful members of the out-of-doors it would be far better to trap one that is doing harm and then release it where it can continue its useful life.

Snappers scrape a hole in a sandy place for their eggs. These are round and white. They are about the size of ping-pong balls and like those balls, they bounce if tossed on the floor.

Of all fresh-water turtles, the snapper is the most important. It is big enough to demand respect for its powerful jaws. It is also big enough for man to desire its delicious flesh. Hotels buy huge numbers of snappers every year and turn them into soup.

The Box Turtle

Of all the turtles in the United States, none is as popular as the box turtle. Its plastron is hinged so it can close its shell completely, covering its head, legs and tail within the horny protection of its little house. The shell closes so tightly that the blade of a sharp knife cannot be inserted. They grow to be four to five inches long.

Box turtles are easy to tame. They learn to feed from the hand and enjoy fruit, berries and bits of raw meat. They appear to accept captivity happily so long as they are given a box of dirt in which they can dig and some shallow water where they can drink and have an occasional good soak. They often live for thirty or forty years. One lived to be 123 years old.

Box turtles are found throughout the eastern states and as far west as central Texas. There are several species. One of the brightest is the Florida box turtle which is quite yellow. The ornate box turtle has the fanciest pattern.

The ornate box turtle lives chiefly on sandy plains and prairies. It likes to burrow in the ground when it is hot. Many people think they are very scarce. Then along comes a heavy rain and suddenly the ornate box turtles which had hidden in the ground seem to be everywhere.

Lizards

Imagine almost any lizard greatly magnified and it would be a monster as strange and terrifying as a dinosaur come to life. Some have big frills or pouches which they can inflate when they wish. Usually these become brightly colored when blown up. Others have enlarged scales or spines so sharp we are glad they are tiny. When some species open their mouths we discover they are lined with vivid colors. The wings of flying lizards are gay as beach umbrellas when open. Many lizards can change color in a few minutes.

Among the 2,500 species of lizards in the world there is not only great variation in color and form but their habits vary as much as their shapes. Most can swim, at least one has learned to run on the surface of the water, many live on land, in trees, or on the desert. A few have learned to glide.

Even among members of a given family of lizards variations are great. Take the monitor lizards of Africa, Asia and Australia. Of these the Komodo dragon, named for the island where it is most common, is the biggest of all lizards. It reaches a length of ten feet and may weigh almost two hundred pounds. Its jaws are powerful and it can swallow almost half a deer at a single gulp. An Australian monitor looks like a miniature Komodo dragon but it never grows longer than ten inches. The Komodo dragon is twelve times as long as the smallest monitor.

Though the biggest lizard is a monitor, the smallest monitor is by no means the smallest lizard. That prize goes to the gecko family which has one member that never grows longer than one and a third inches.

Komodo Dragon

Glass Lizard or Glass Snake

Many people make pets of geckos, particularly the larger species. They are good insect-catchers in houses which they search at night. Geckos have sticky pads on their feet and can run up walls and over ceilings as easily as a fly. Their squeaky cry sounds like *geck-o.*

Lizards vary all the way from having four long, strong legs to having none at all. The longest lizard in the United States is the glass lizard (often called glass snake), which has no legs at all. No wonder they are mistaken for snakes! When frightened, a glass lizard sheds its loose tail, which is usually longer than its head and body together. A new tail grows quickly but it is never as long or perfect as the first one. Many species of lizards, like the glass snake, shed the tail, which immediately wriggles violently. An enemy watches the wriggling tail and the lizard escapes.

In India there is a foot-long spiny-tailed lizard with long sharp spines on the tip of its tail. It digs burrows eight or nine feet long. There it hides and on cold nights it closes the entrance. Snakes like to eat lizards but if one enters the burrow, the spiny-tail turns its tail toward the entrance and shakes the tip violently. Any snake or small mammal hurries out of the hole at once.

In the tropics of Australia is a frilled lizard that reaches a length of three feet. A frill or cape can be inflated on each side of its neck until it is nine or ten inches across. At the same time the lizard opens its mouth widely to show a lining of brightest yellow while a pair of enlarged teeth make it look ferocious. It hisses loudly and is an alarming sight. But the frilled lizard is only bluffing, for it is completely harmless.

Fringed Lizard

Ancient people imagined a horrible monster they called a basilisk. It was so frightful that its hissing was supposed to drive away all reptiles. If a man looked at it he would be turned to stone.

When the yard-long tree lizards of Central and South America were discovered they were so fantastic that the name "basilisk" was given to them. Male basilisks are green and brown with dark cross bars. A reddish crest along the back can be raised or lowered at will while a membrane on the back of the head can be inflated into a big upright flap. Usually basilisks live in trees that hang over water. When frightened

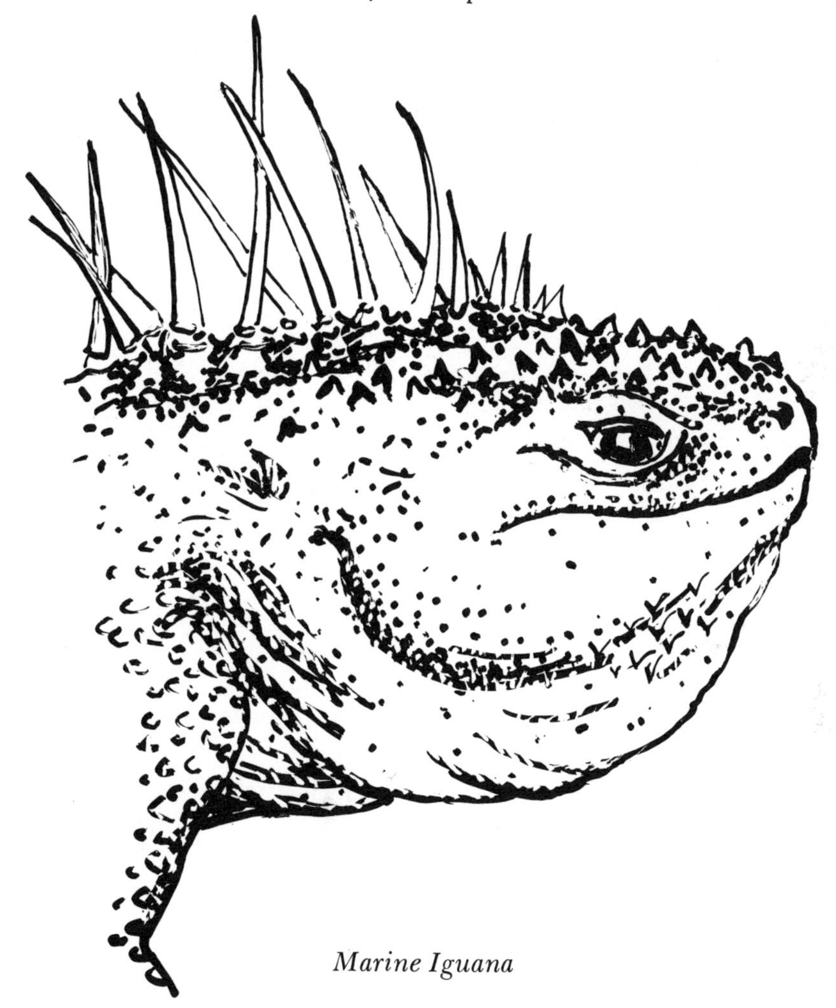

Marine Iguana

they drop suddenly to the water and run rapidly over the surface on their hind legs. The long tail acts as a rudder.

The imaginary basilisks of ancient people were terrible creatures. True-life basilisks may look as strange as those mythical creatures but they are perfectly harmless.

Iguanas form one large family of American lizards. All have long tails and those of large species are eaten by people in Central and South America. Their beautiful skins are used for shoes and handbags. They are good swimmers yet they climb trees easily.

The Galápagos iguana is the strangest member of this family. It eats seaweed. As the tide begins to fall, these marine iguanas gather along the shore. Sometimes they become so impatient they dive through the surf for a mouthful of seaweed. In all the world, these are the only lizards that find their food in the ocean.

Of all strange lizards, the true chameleon of Africa which changes color so rapidly that "chameleon" has come to mean changeableness, takes the prize. A chameleon has a blunt head. Its body is so thin it looks as if it had been rolled flat and then stood on edge. Its toes look like tweezers. Its long tail is usually curled into a tight shell-like coil when it is not wrapped like a monkey's tail around a twig. Its eyes bulge out on little turrets that can be swiveled separately in any direction. While one eye swings forward, the other may turn backward.

Most lizards move with flashing speed. Chameleons move with astonishing slowness. They are especially funny when fighting or courting. Then their actions look like a slow-motion movie.

The tongue of a chameleon is almost unbelievable. It has a sticky tip and acts like a popgun. It is longer than the head and body combined. The chameleon stalks its prey. When still far from it, it suddenly shoots out its tongue faster than the eye can follow and presto — the insect is caught on the sticky tip and swallowed.

When chameleons stalk their prey, they keep their thin edge toward it so they look like a leaf. But when they fight with another chameleon they turn broadside to their enemy and make themselves look as large and terrifying as possible.

From the huge Komodo-dragon to the smallest gecko, from the changeable chameleons to the spiny-tails, from the iguanas to Gila monsters, there is always enchantment and surprise in store for those who study lizards.

A Basilisk with its long tail and a Horned Toad

The Horned Lizard

Horned lizards look as if they had been crushed, for they are flat and round as a pancake. They are found all the way from Guatemala to south central Canada but they are most common in the deserts of the American Southwest. Horned lizards are softly colored and match the desert. Patches and spots of yellow, black, brown and gray on their spiny skins make them blend into the earth so they are almost invisible until they move. They can run with great speed.

Sometimes when a horned lizard is angry, it puffs itself up like a toad (they are often called horned toads) and suddenly shoots from bulging eyes a jet of blood many times as far as it is long.

Horned lizards are covered with pointed horny scales and bristles like the spines of cactus. Most species have horns on the snout and on the back of the head. The abdomens of some are edged with more spines. They are so horny and prickly we are glad they are tiny, not the size of the dinosaur Triceratops which they resemble in miniature.

These lizards are particularly fond of ants. Many a person who discovers a horned lizard captures it and holds it gently until he finds the nearest anthill. When the small captive is placed on the anthill it instantly forgets its fright and begins to eat ants greedily as they swarm out of the hill.

The Gila Monster

In all the world only two lizards are known to be poisonous, though a species in Borneo is suspected of being dangerous, for it is closely related to the two poisonous American lizards. Both those lizards live in Mexico but one, the Gila (pronounced *he-la*) monster is found as far north as Arizona.

The Gila monster, which seldom becomes more than eighteen inches long, is very stocky and strong. Lying on the desert sand it looks like a gay piece of pink and black Indian beadwork. Its jaws gape widely to show white teeth in a pitch-black mouth.

In the hot dry country where they live, Gila monsters are quick and agile. They snap with the fury of an angry dog. Once their powerful jaws have clamped on a hand or leg it is almost impossible to pry them apart. They keep their grip even if the head is chopped off. As the jaws seize an enemy in their viselike grip, poison flows from glands in the lower jaws along grooves in the back teeth and is forced into the wound. The poison can kill a man. It is said that about 20 per cent of the people bitten by a Gila monster die.

Oddly enough, pet Gila monsters are sluggish. They are not recommended as pets for there is always a chance that they will suddenly bite their caretakers.

Gila Monster

Gila monsters lay anywhere from five to thirteen eggs, which they hide in damp sand. In about thirty days the four-inch-long young hatch.

Like a few other desert dwellers, Gila monsters store excess fat as food. Unlike the camel, which stores its excess fat in a hump, Gila monsters store theirs in the tail. When temperatures are high and food is plentiful, their tails grow thick and fat. This fat is gradually absorbed by the body when it is cold or food is scarce.

The Green Anole

In the United States reef geckos are the smallest lizards, glass lizards have no legs, Gila monsters are poisonous, but green anoles are best known, for many of them are sold as pets. Green anoles are found in all the states bordering the Gulf of Mexico and as far north as Virginia.

Green anoles seldom reach more than seven inches in length, and of that about 2/3 is the long thin tail. The toes on each foot have adhesive pads which enable them to run up smooth walls. They often drop out of trees or off walls and scamper away unhurt. They move so swiftly it is difficult to catch them except when they are asleep.

These small lizards are often called chameleons though they are not related to the true chameleons of Africa. However, in less than three minutes they can change from leaf-green to brown. This change is usually caused by fright, anger, or a temperature change. It is not an attempt to match the color on which they stand. When cold, angry or frightened they usually turn green. On a hot sunny day they are most likely to be a rich brown.

Green anoles have a loose flap of skin on the throat which they can inflate into a good-sized fan. At courting time or when they wish to frighten away another anole, they do amusing push-ups with their front legs, bobbing the head as they do so while the fan on the throat grows large and bright rosy pink.

The Broad-headed Skink

Skinks are so glossy, smooth and quick that they are difficult to catch and hold. Even if you think you have one you may find you are holding nothing but a long wriggling tail while the lizard has escaped. Large skinks can bite hard enough to give a good pinch.

The broad-headed skink found from Pennsylvania to Florida and west to Texas is the largest of the many skinks in the United States. Some of them become a foot long.

Young broad-headed skinks are often called blue-tailed skinks. Then their black body is lined with bright yellow stripes and their tail is brightest blue. As they grow older, the males turn olive brown. Their cheeks bulge and their heads turn bright red.

Throughout the South adult broad-headed skinks are often called red-headed scorpions and they are greatly feared. Really they are completely harmless and since their food is insects, they must be considered good friends of man.

Snakes

Say "reptile" and most people instantly think of snakes. Yet snakes are newcomers to the world of reptiles. They are the youngest of that group of animals.

No living snake has legs. Their form is smooth and slender. They

Bushmaster

Cobra

have no external ears and it is believed they cannot hear. They have no eyelids and their sight is fairly poor. Their long forked tongue fits in a sheath in the lower jaw when it is not extended to investigate its surroundings. The tongue cannot sting or give off poison. It is as harmless as a human tongue.

The jaws of snakes are remarkable. The lower one is divided in halves which can be pushed apart. Therefore snakes can swallow objects larger around than they are.

Snakes do not live nearly as long as man. It is doubtful if many live more than twenty years though one anaconda in captivity lived twenty-eight years.

The longest snake known is a reticulate python of Asia which measured thirty-two feet. A South American anaconda measured thirty feet. A rock python of Africa measured twenty-five feet, while an amethystine python of Australia measured twenty-one feet.

About 5 per cent of the snakes of the world are poisonous yet those few cause most men to fear all snakes. The king cobra of southern Asia is the longest poisonous snake, having reached a length of eighteen feet four inches. The black mamba with an extreme length of fourteen feet is the longest poison snake of Africa. In South America the bushmaster reaches twelve feet, while Australia's tiapan at eleven feet holds the record for that continent. No man bitten by a tiapan, fortunately very rare, has been known to recover. The diamondback rattlesnake of North America has reached eight feet and is probably the heaviest poison snake for its length.

Of the two thousand snakes in the world, the worm snakes are the smallest. They look like worms and like worms they burrow in the earth where they lay their eggs, which are the size of cooked rice. None is poisonous. Although called blind, it is believed they can tell the difference between light and darkness.

Lizards are bluffers but snakes are even better at that game. Many harmless snakes vibrate their tails. Rattlers which are not bluffing do this best. Many snakes raise the head and flatten the neck to frighten enemies. The poisonous cobras have brought this to the peak of development. Some snakes hiss loudly and others make threatening jabs with their heads. Most snakes like to avoid danger rather than fight. Some, like the garter snakes, give off a bad-smelling musk if handled, some hide the head under the body, some roll into tight balls, and others become rigid.

Not a single vegetable-eating snake is known in the whole world. Although snakes can eat large objects, they prefer long slim creatures since everything they eat must be swallowed whole. They have no way to tear it apart. Their back-slanting teeth help to force food into the throat. A snake twenty-five feet long can swallow a mammal weighing seventy-five pounds, or about half the weight of the snake. After eating a large meal, a snake can scarcely move. Many of the biggest snakes are killed when they are sluggish after a big meal. It is not surprising that the favorite food of many snakes is another snake, for it is easiest to swallow. There is not a single authentic case of a full-grown man being swallowed by a snake.

Of all its senses, that of smell is keenest. It is said that many snakes trail their victims using the tongue as well as the nose. Many people believe large snakes hide beside animal trails and ambush their prey.

Some snakes bear live young which are never given any attention by the mother. Some egg-laying snakes coil around their eggs and many species stay near them as if to protect them.

All snakes swim easily. Certain ones called sea snakes live in or near the ocean. They are closely related to the poisonous coral snakes and seldom measure more than four feet. They are found only in the Eastern Hemisphere. There are many fresh-water snakes in the United States but all of these are harmless except the cottonmouths. Many snakes climb easily and some seldom or never come down to earth. On some Asiatic islands the golden tree snake is called a flying snake. It does not really fly but flattens its body and makes long leaps from tree to tree.

Perhaps because so many people are afraid of snakes they believe silly stories about them. Repeatedly people claim mother snakes swallow their young when danger threatens. Snakes often swallow other snakes but to eat, not protect them! One widely held belief is that snakes "charm" their victims, including men, so they are powerless to escape. One of the most amusing of such tales is a story by William Henry Hudson in which gauchos (cowboys of South America) told him of a huge snake that charmed a rabbit so it could not run away but was drawn backward right into the open mouth of the snake. The gauchos actually believed that story but thought Hudson was lying when he told them about subway trains that ran underground.

Many people believe snakes do not die until sunset, that coachwhip snakes whip bad children, that the tongue of a snake can sting and that milk snakes milk cows. They even believe in such impossible stories as that the hoop snake takes its tail in its mouth and rolls after its victim, which it kills with a stinger in the tip of the tail. Perhaps you know other snake stories which have no truth in them.

Snakes are pleasant to handle, for their smooth dry scales, sinewy muscles and handsome patterns can be most enjoyed at close range. They may be brought home for a few days and kept in a dry cage furnished with a few branches on which to climb and a dish of water for drinking. It is best to release them in a few days if they do not accept food readily. Naturally it is important before picking up snakes to know which ones in an area are poisonous. Do not handle poisonous snakes, ever, not even when they are dead.

Snakes are among the most interesting and useful animals in any community and should be enjoyed and understood by the people who live there. Unfortunately man is the worst enemy of snakes. Great numbers of valuable and harmless snakes are killed on highways every year by thoughtless people who will not slow down and give snakes a chance. Other harmless snakes are killed by well-meaning people who cannot tell a harmless, useful snake from the few poisonous ones in the United States.

The Coral Snake

This little snake that seldom grows longer than thirty inches is as bright as a string of shiny red, yellow and black beads. Unlike the thick-bodied, ugly, triangular-headed snake most people believe all poisonous species to be, the coral snake is slim and there is little more division between its neck and black head than there is in an earthworm. As it moves across a lawn it looks as innocent as an earthworm but far more beautiful.

Strangely enough there are some harmless snakes that not only look very much like a coral snake but behave like them. Two of these, the scarlet snake and the scarlet king snake, both with red, not black, snouts, may be found in the same gardens with coral snakes. All of these snakes like to burrow in the earth and are most likely to come to the surface after a heavy rain, on dull days, or at dusk.

Coral snakes are found from eastern North Carolina to Argentina. They do not appear dangerous until frightened. Then they throw themselves about in a strange way and may lash out fiercely. There are many tales of people who have picked them up and handled coral snakes and even carried them in their pockets without harm. In spite of such stories it must be remembered that the poison of coral snakes is as dangerous as that of a cobra, a mamba or a tiger snake.

Instead of hollow teeth like a rattler, coral snakes have small grooved teeth. Like a Gila monster, the coral snake chews when it bites, forcing poison from its glands down grooves and so into the wound. Few people bitten by coral snakes recover. On the other hand, very few people have been bitten by a coral snake unless they handled it carelessly or teased it.

The Rattlesnake

There are about thirty species of rattlesnakes ranging from the pigmy of less than two feet to the diamondback, which may reach eight feet. Unless the tip of the tail has been chopped off, all species have rattles. Their age cannot be told by the number of rattles. If sufficient food is obtained, from two to four rattles are added each year. Each new rattle or button is added to the string unless it is broken or worn off.

All rattlers can inject enough poison in a bite to cause an unpleasant wound. The bigger ones can cause death unless immediate medical help is given. People who hike in rattlesnake country should wear high boots and carry snake-bite kits. When climbing they should be careful not to place their hands on ledges where a rattler may be

Diamond Back Rattlesnake

resting. Caution should be the watchword where rattlers are common.

Rattlers do not always give warning when approached though if awake they usually do so. They prefer to retreat rather than attack. They never jump or spring completely off the ground at a person. If forced to attack they can strike about a third of their length. The other two-thirds remains on the ground. Two long hollow fangs are driven into the flesh with great power. Poison flows through the hollow fangs and into the wound.

The King Snake

One day in a small Florida town a boy shouted, "A king snake is eating a rattler by the big live oak."

Everybody ran to watch. The king snake had thrown coils around the rattler and was beginning to swallow it. The people were delighted for children often played beneath the big tree.

King snakes do not especially seek poison snakes when hungry. They are not affected by the poison of any American snake. Therefore if they meet one when hungry, they do not hesitate to attack. King snakes also eat many rats, and mice. Farmers often keep them as pets in their barns and gardens.

In spring female king snakes lay about two dozen eggs. The young ones, which are from nine to twelve inches long when they come out of their two-inch-long shells may reach a length of eighty-two inches.

Pet king snakes quickly become gentle and appear to enjoy the warmth of human hands. Many a boy has found it amusing to let his pet king snake wrap itself around his waist and then put its head out between the buttons of his shirt. This frightens people who do not know how friendly and useful king snakes are.

The Hog-nosed Snake

Of all the snakes in North America, hog-nosed snakes, which seldom grow longer than twenty inches, are the biggest bluffers. They have frightened so many people with their bluffing that such names as puff adder, spreading adder, hissing adder, blow viper and hissing viper have been given to them.

When alarmed a hog-nosed snake flattens itself suddenly so bright new colors are revealed. It looks as deadly as a cobra. It hisses and

Hog-nosed Snake

strikes, but with its mouth closed tightly. If this does not frighten you away, it may act as if dying, writhe about with its mouth open and its tongue trailing in the dust. Slowly the writhing may stop and the snake rests on its back as if dead. If you turn it over, it will flip onto its back as if a dead snake must lie that way. No snake is more amusing than a bluffing hog-nosed snake. They have never been known to bite. If you take one home it soon becomes tame and will not bluff.

Hog-nosed snakes are dull and dusty looking. They are thick-bodied and have tilted snouts. It is said the upturned snout is a help in burrowing in the ground after toads, their favorite food.

The Garter Snake

Garter snakes occur from the Atlantic to the Pacific and from the Gulf of Mexico to Canada. All garter snakes are striped, usually with three or more yellow stripes running down the back and sides. The brightest species are called ribbon snakes. Sometimes they are called garden snakes for they are found in gardens, in cities as well as the country.

During the winter garter snakes hibernate. They emerge when warmth returns to the earth. Their chief food is earthworms, toads and insects.

In late summer the female gives birth to young garter snakes. There may be anywhere from fifteen to thirty in a single brood. Probably many of the young are eaten by other snakes and birds before they have a chance to grow up.

All garter snakes are harmless. Sometimes if a large one is handled carelessly it will bite because it is frightened. It does not hurt for its teeth are small. A snake should always be handled gently and permitted to hang onto your fingers or wrist. Then it feels safe.

People who watch reptiles and learn to understand them find a new and wonderful world. It is a strange world of animals which have lived on earth far longer than man. Yet so few people have studied these wonderful animals, the reptiles, that new and unknown adventures and knowledge await those who watch and learn about them.

Garter Snake

INDEX

Index